As promised "Music in Stone"
with special emphasis on
page 6.-7.

Love Phyllis.

Music in Stone

A Collection of Poems

Maureen Perkins

GW00544371

Boland Press

First published in 2013
Copyright @ Maureen Perkins

Boland Press
Grove Mill
Hollyfort
Co. Wexford
http://bolandpress.blogspot.com

A CIP catalogue record for this book
is available from the British Library

ISBN: 978-1-907855-06-1

Cover photograph by Brendan Cullen
www.fotos.ie

Cover design by Boland Press

Printed in Ireland by
SPRINT-Print

For Joe

Acknowledgement is given to the following publications where some of these poems, or versions of them, have appeared:

Bray Arts Journal, Strands of Silk, Space Inside Arts Magazine, Poets' Shed (DVD), Tidings, High Tide, Rising Tide, Strands of Silk, and on RTE and LMFM Radio.

Linger, see the skylark soar
find peace in flower and stone

The Burren

Maureen Perkins lives in Drogheda, Co. Louth. She is a founder member of Bealtaine Writers in Dublin and a member of The Shed Poets Society, Dalkey.

In 2007, Maureen was awarded an MA in Creative Writing from The Seamus Heaney Centre for Poetry, Queen's University, Belfast.

Music in Stone is her first book of poetry.

Contents

Music in Stone

Wicklow Man

You were born in this valley
constant and solid like stone
early taught to till the earth
to care for sheep heavy with lamb
drive cattle to Blessington mart.

At night you heard farmers' talk
of weather, births and deaths
soaring costs, Michael Dwyer
and what the neighbour's
squinting window saw.

You learned the art of make and mend
found you had creative hands
your granite stones grew into walls
in time your walls grew into homes.

Batchelors' Walk

It's an uphill walk from
the Toll Inn to Walter's Mill,
a stony lane braced by rock
steep banks
dripping water.

In the haggard
ragwort hides a rusty plough.
The old house listens
to a meitheal swapping
a day to the threshing.

They gather at the Inn,
heads over pints
stalling their hunger,
moon-mocked, trudging home
on barren boreens.

Husbandry

This storied land is part of you –
croppies hanged on Dunlavin Green,
Freney the highwayman whose
horse shoes face backwards;

from grandfather Arthur you learned young
when to plant and plough
where to find a straying lamb,
how to make and mend a fence.

They'll break out at some gap
if they find a weakness, you say.
Hoisting the crowbar, you ram a post-hole,
test with your eye.

To the rhythm of hammer and bend
you sink arrowed posts in dank clay,
tease and staple a length of sheep wire
in this wild basin surrounded by hills.

Away on Lug the heather is lurid purple.
I watch you falter
feel the pain in your arthritic knee.

Blessington Lakes

The Liffey drops
from hill to lowland
Russellstown to Russborough
Blessington to Broadleas,
acres of grassland.

Ballinahown to Ballyknockan
Valleymount to Lackan,
the poor cluster on thin soil
dream a flock of breeding ewes
two mares to plough.

Stints give each a share
in fields and commons:
Bleaching Field, Murphy's Inch,
Limekiln Field, Under the Sallies,
summer grazing in collops.

When they heard their
land would be flooded
they took it very hard
Cromwell all over again.
Is there nothing we can do

to save our father's land
our graveyard, our holy well,
the High Field, the Middle Field,
the field forninth the door.

One man clings to home
till waters quench the fire,
float settlebed and dresser
his father' s blackthorn stick
squeal of pig, bawl of calf.

Music in Stone
i.m. Mary Davis Harney

To the rhythm of wedge,
sledge and crowbar, quarrymen
split grey-white granite,
its grain aligned east west
with the rising sun.
Foxgloves shiver.

Stonecutters chisel and punch.
They taper and shape millstone,
lintel, pier topped with pineapple,
troughs for forge and farmyard.

The gaffer likes to hear them hum
while the mallet moves faster.
Ballyknockan sings
to the chip-chip of the pick
and the schoolmaster plays
the bagpipes.

Foxglove

She shivers
in a granite cleft
her chorus of bells
on bee alert
like pink visages
open to propagate.

Vintage

The Big House is a skeleton
spilling gardens into fields.
Gnarled trees parade clusters
of damsons on scraggy twigs.

We bite blue-black skin
sink teeth in warm ochre flesh
that melts on our tongues
spit stones on spongy soil,
spatter purple.

Damsons plonk into buckets
we fill for the wine press,
hour by hour oozings ferment,
casks of siphoned ruby wine
hibernate like bears in wìnter.

Harry

Cartwheels crunch
on cobbled path
horse hooves ring
between the shafts.

Every day
feed the pigs
milk the cows
feed the suck calf.

Down the yard
body angled
he carries swill
to empty troughs,

shoulders hunched
he holds a bucket
of spilling milk
to the stubborn calf

thinks of his son
who threw down
a pitch-fork in the rain
never to make hay again.

Feathers

She sits in her apron of calico
in slanting winter light, her shrewd
eyes survey the women waiting
in a chorus of chatter.

Men stoop through the doorway
carrying birds dripping blood,
lay them at her feet an offering
to the goddess of plenty.
Don't let the turkeys grow cold, they say,

as lightening fingers pluck feathers
falling in drifts on a carpet of down.
By nightfall a year's work
hangs from the rafters like
ranks of bare-chested soldiers.

Landscape County Wicklow
after Evie Hone

You went to Wicklow a lively way
angled your brush to the hills,
painted a patchwork of black-fenced fields,
a framed celebration, like windows.

The ploughman guides two Clydesdales
slices deep the rich clay,
creates lush furrows hungry for seed,
the scene not changed since Nineveh.

Clarke's perfect plug

He sits at table, tense
to get to the end of his meal.

Penknife ready he scrapes
the bowl of his crooked pipe,
tap tap on the heel of his boot
until the dross falls out.

Knife angled, he cuts tobacco
into his cupped hand,
kneads pungent pieces in his palm,
fills the bowl with luscious flakes.

After five strikes,
pulls and puffs
to light the pipe,
a red glow and calm smoke rises.

Rue

What hurts
is the bent
sadness
in your back
as you dig
the clay
driven
to bury
your dreams.

Mirror mirror on the wall

1

My baby's face is not snow-white
her hair is more the raven's wing
but I smell roses in her skin.

Now a brooding hen my daughter
forgets she never wanted children –
no more worry about kith and kin.

Two eyes drawn from ultrasound
moon-morsel cradled in a bubble
you are the fairest of us all.

2

Shadows cross my daughter's face
the hardest days we've ever spent
no power on earth can wake

our child from her eternal sleep
face quiescent, stoic, deep.
I cry. How white the winter is.

We hold our snow-white, say goodbye
her cradle now a casket,
a red rose, wreaths of gorse
yellow on the Blackemore.

Ring-a-ring-a-rosy

Knee-high at our front door, I spy
my stretchy face in the shiny knob.
People go up and down Green Street
passing the Freemasons' place, always
locked. No one looks in there, the devil
is inside. By the castle wall on Rosse Row
girls are playing ring-a-ring-a-rosy.

Grownups stop at our house. Through
the dark hallway I hear footsteps upstairs,
creaks on the landing, then out into the light
my father carries a white box
like a huge iced cake.

My cousin runs to me and whispers
your baby brother is in the box.
She holds my hand and we skip away
singing ring-a-ring-a-rosy.

15

The Wedding Guest

He holds his hand high
blows invisible smoke in the air
pulls a photograph
from behind his back.

Look at you smoking
like a trooper. And drinking
lashings of wine, I bet.
You look well there
but look at you now.

I remember the banter,
the sunshine, the misery.
You looked into my eyes
and you knew.

Your first love was Drogheda

Were you to walk today
you would find your way
among the narrow streets
hidden lanes and byways
your father's hat shop
St. Peter's bell pealing for prayer.

Always the Robinson Crusoe
by the river traffic on the quay
your boat plied the green
waves of the Boyne to poach
salmon or shoot duck
feeding on the sloblands.

Rambling the Mornington seashore
thyme covering the sandbanks
you watched the white winged terns
and the oystercatchers feed
about the mussel beds hearing
the weird call of the curlew.

You paint, 'Baltry on the River Boyne'
peasants in their boats and fields
always a compassionate eye
catching an innate melancholy.

Retrieving my walled town

See Millmount, de Lacy's castlemotte,
Hugh's head rests in St. Thomas'
his headless trunk at Bective Abbey
below shimmers Spenser's pleasant Boyne.

Pass the chandlers, hear the clamour
on the wharf, ships load up to ply
their wares from Iceland to the Levant.
Smell the herring, livestock and hide.

Walk by the Bullring, the Tholsel and
The Cornmarket's arcade of butter
and grain, its weathervane a plough
a sickle, a sheaf of wheat.

Potters mart at Besexwell lane,
hand-built and kiln fired cookpots,
wheelthrown jugs and pipkins pink
to hard fired orange glaze.

St. Magdalene's Priory rims Sunday's Gate
inlaid tiles pave cloister and aisle,
noble and holyman are buried here
a six foot female lies in archbishop's grave.

Droichead Átha

Early morning hangs over
de Lacy's walled town.

A bell that rang
for work or prayer
stays silent now
in Magdalene Tower.

The Tholsel clock chimes,
church bells ring out
in Georgian streets.
Gothic steeples soar.

Echoes of Cromwell's
cannonade rumble on Millmount,
drown in the dark water
of the river Boyne.

Auction Rooms

Across the narrow street
a chapel's stained glass
window blazes kingfisher
blue in the blue morning.

A kitchen table carried
out to Duke Street
collects the light
like amber
winking yellow tints.

Now this beech table
is mine, its dovetailed
drawers for odds and ends.

Monasterboice

See the Round Tower
hear monks sound
their handbells
and rain soft on your face
walk on rough grass
between grave stones.

Muiredeach's Cross
writes a book in stone,
chisels cartoons
of pagan and holy writ
two cats in high relief
on its shaft content
in a shrine of stone.

Passage Grave
i.m. Bettina Poeschel

Going Bettina's way to Newgrange,
a ridgeline down to the Boyne,
a tomb's mouth in dazzlewhite quartz
swallows the stillness of a winter day.

I join new age pilgrims at a kiosk
huddled hoods and padded anoraks
talking of where she was found
over the river near Donore.

Like rabbits in a narrow burrow
we squeeze through the passage of stone,
stand in a recessed burial chamber
risen high, a corbelled cone.

As effigies we wait in dimness.
I feel the glimmer of the axeman's flint
on ripples, diamonds, spirals, zigzags
picked and pointed on giant slabs.

Bettina never reached Dagda's mound,
last resting place of druids and kings
her killer hid her in a thicket of thorn
a prey to birdlife as she lay alone.

She will not be here at winter solstice
to see the light of the new born sun
creep over the river through frozen fields
flood the tomb in a gilded stream.

Derinish

Sun melts a mist
of trees in Killykeen
by Lough Oughter's shore
glimpses a trinity of islands.

A sessile oak budbursts
sucking light from the sky,
drooping catkins offer nectar
to the bee at noon.

I touch smooth bark of ash
sacred to Setanta
hear the lash and swish
on breathless hurling pitch.

A red squirrel and a hedgehog
rustle in leaf mould,
reed-warblers mating song
excites the spring.

Doves

Down the dripping lane to the hazel wood
I stop, startled as two pigeons burst
from a tree, exploding skywards.
My eye follows their smack and flap.

They plunge onto a green-grass clearing,
step ungainly in a fantail flare,
side-step, waddle a dance apart,
come close to coo and nibble.

On white-wing flash they fly to roost
in a shower-drenched cypress tree.
Puffball breasts thrust out, they
nod and natter, peck and patter.

Down the dripping lane today
blood marks a breast, a black eye stares.

Poets' Shed

Granite steps in cliff face
lead me to a timbered shed
where poems are dovetailed.

Wind carves the waves
a sand-grained stone tastes salty.
I stroke planed curve

of blue dolphin
lift a conch to my ear
listen to another sea.

Evie Hone

Versed in the art of monument and manuscript
you tap new aspect of mason and scribe
dig deep in your treasure house of artefacts
see riches in stained glass at Chartres.

Sketching from carved stone crosses
whimsical miniatures of bell and book
fired by the need to illuminate
nothing deters your search for light.

Grief
after Jack B Yeats

The question is
what is the cause of grief.

A redcoat, fear rearing
in the eye of his charger,
rides roughshod over
a hooded birdbeaked mass
trapped in the street.

Heads clutched
in blue drapes
bleed cadmium yellow,
a smokepit belches.

The answer is shrouded
in an ashen pall.

The Burren

Not Praeger's dried skeleton
more Yeats' hills of agate and jade
celebrate limestone in infinite space
a mythic brooding moonscape,

scailps like terraced rock gardens,
amphibious rivers above and below
through the dripping limestone dark,
hear their springs, music of Orpheus.

Poulnabrone dolmen rears its pagan
head, a place of the dead
on plateau of tinkling pavements,
blue gentian, mossy saxifrage.

Linger, see the skylark soar
find peace in flower and stone.

She chose the Rose

You live in oracle song
arouse the wisdom of sages
whose stories sing
in the lilt of your pen.

Through your epics
Cú Chulainn stalks
in rhyme upon rhyme
a hero alive in the Táin.

Maude Gonne at Howth station
you knelt at her feet
but her heart only listened
to a marching beat.

William Orpen
after Michael Hartnett

Greedy in that he overvalued riches
generous in the sense he shared his art
with eager students, knew that
what passed for patriotism was often
away with the fairies. Nevertheless
he loved his country, clenched his hands
around his world as he found it.

He was night that craved the light.
He was fashion in high places.
He was a caricaturist of the famous.
He was a caricaturist of himself.
He was the Pepys of the Western Front.
He was the tears of a war to end wars.
He was the tears of a war that didn't end wars.

Fire on his pen

Bernard Shaw digests Shakespeare
in a Synge Street basement kitchen,
mother plays the piano upstairs,
father in wholesale
(retail out of the question)
blows his trombone,
aunt Shah plucks a harp
an uncle makes his bugle moo.

Quizzical eyebrows
sarcastic nostrils of Gounod's fiend
finds his Dublin base and ludicrous,
Shaw packs a carpet bag
boards the north wall boat
finds England a hell hole.
But isn't he the small devil who
frescoed Mephistopheles on a Dalkey wall.

Not to take a risk a greater risk.
With more devilment than prudence,
fire on his pen,
born to criticise, banned for excess
he speaks to the world obsessively
unlike Saint Joan and Socrates,
too crafty to burn at the stake
or drink hemlock, a Pygmalion
in love with the statue he makes.

Roger Casement to Alice

If only they had landed me in Connemara
armed comrades waited for me there.

Through the kindness of Emmerline
and some Irish friends
we shall help the plight of children
in houses, the worst ever seen.

Money hidden at the old fort,
near Banna Strand,
is for the school at Carraroe,
a meal a day for every child,
there shall be grace in Irìsh
before and a song after.

The war gave me qualms,
the concentration camps bigger ones.
Up in lonely Congo forests where I found
Leopold's heart of darkness
I was looking at black tragedy
in the eyes of another race.

Whatever good I have done
I carry from my own country,
willing to do my part
wherever it leads me.

Rathlin

On the sea journey between
Antrim and Argyle an island tells
stories of Bruce and the spider,
the defeat of Bonny Prince Charlie,
Richard Branson's drop-down balloon.

Moby Dick spray on the
ferry boat swirls currents
boiling underneath. Look out
on basalt cliffs, pink in the sunset,
greetings of strangers at Port an Draighlin.

Invasion and famine
created the island people,
upper end Gaelic, as wild
and untamed as the puffins,
Scots to the south in bible grasp.

Poets gather in The Manor House
sing stories of haunting
Ceannann Dubh, Fionnula
in the storm sea of Moyle,
Roger Casement, Louis MacNeice

the letter

a stone stuns
the head sits normal
nerves numb
the taut heart asks
robot feet move round
a wooden way
blind east west
words fall like lead.

Sirocco

When east wind mocks the April sun
pelts spears down my back
sheering silver light

I recoil into a cloak of cloud
simulate a smile
waver on.

Each year the spear
bleeds through.
Thawed, I will endure.

Peaceable Kingdom Lost

'By right of conquest say the Paxton Boys
kill every Indian in ye Barracks,
extirpate the vermin, scalp bounties
for every Indian we kill.'

Blue moonlight slides skeletal
tree in Pennsylvania, shadowing
Indians on the leaf path
soft-footing to Conestoga Creek.

The Quaker, Penn, their Onas,
whose bond on parchment and words
were held in tribal trust,
a belt of wampum to bury their axe.

The workhouse massacre haunts,
their birth right stolen,
their dreaming bones cry out
a death-dirge on strings of wampum.

Lost people of Anatolia

Sun-baked houses of brick and stone
glow apricot in terracotta heat,
kilims weave orange and rose.

Flanked by sculpted lions, a gate
opens a city of lime-white courts,
merchants barter copper and grain.

A royal tomb is circled by rings of stone.
An axe, a spear, a goblet of gold
rest with the bones of the dead.

Hazel Lavery

Slim like a willow
standing sylvan in
Dublin's Municipal Gallery.

She is romantic Ireland
a ballad yet to be sung
a dream yet to be won.

Red Rose

Lady of the night, overblown,
thorns jag your wilted neck
your gown falls in tatters
your moonface shatters
bees hurry to another bloom.

Once jostling for the limelight
tight-budded, heavy scented
on breast of ball gown
you danced till dawn.

Scarlet lady where is your bloom.

St. Brigid

Goddess of a thousand charms
she gives the heifer
lustre of a swan.

Golden-haired bride of the kine
her hue like cotton grass
her bird the linnet
the oystercatcher her guile,

deity of the house
born neither within nor without,
her cross a sunwheel, she brings
the wheeling of the cosmos
from darkness to light.

When the lark gets a new voice
on Brigid's day, the raven
should have a nest
an egg by Shrove
and a chick by Easter.

Lime wash the house on Brigid's Eve,
Brideog carry strawbaby
from door to door, strawboys
pipe from house to house.

Drop the crios of plaited straw
over heads and bodies,
step from the golden ring.

The Mill on the Fane
for Patrick Kavanagh

A bay mare rolls, spreadeagles
on the bank of the fast-flowing Fane
the blackbird turns his note at a right angle
in the garden of the golden apples.

Niagarous mill-race spins the flywheel
feeds corn from kiln to crusher
flour flows silent into sacks of hessian
I listen to the mill of the golden grain.

The millhouse sags in shadow
chestnuts snap on cartwheel track
horses feed, there's talk of oats
flax and every blooming thing.

Poppies' paper blouses

To Yarrow to Yarrow
friends flock
hats bob
stag suits strut
flaming poppies rock.

Men in tartan
flick their kilts
women totter on pins
hug each other in pain
poppies yawn disdain.

In horse and carriage
bride and groom
go clippity clop,
popping poppies pop.

The Dancer

He came from the lake
hair black as the knave of spades
lived in a drowned field
under the sallies.

Natives amazed at his dash
on the dance floor, swooping
a girl off her feet
into the bend of a foxtrot.

She buried her face in his curls
swooned at her daring,
threw her arms in the air
trance-dancing.

Mothers went into hysterics
hid their daughters in furze,
stories of a cloven hoof
vanishing under the floorboards.

Críona

She weaves skeins of love
with slender thread
a lace world of white.

Bobbins lace a pattern,
whole stitch, half stitch, twist,
gimp start, single gimp, gimp finish.

Bobbin beads have names
Dolly Varden, Kitty Fisher,
Ostrich Plume and Evil Eye,

Butterfly and Bird Edge
pillows light as cloud
sailing above the lough.

He longs for lost energy

We measure and map
under the dormer roof
to offer an extension.

As he tongues and grooves
strips of pitch pine
his flushed face alarms.

Lifting frail fingers
he lays and grouts a wall
of opaque glass brick.

Borrowed skylight sun
slants through
to heal and restore.

The Wave

You're welcome Mia smiles
as she ladles her Thai beef curry into bowls.
She is happy to be here
for her first grandchild's birth.
Liah her daughter, settled here now,
glides among guests in peacock silk.

Home again in Phuket,
Mia walks her beloved beach
sits in palm tree shade.
A muffled sound
the tide sucked out,
a wall of water pauses
thunders to the shore.

Liah combs the lists.

Chopin

Tell me how
you capture sound, weave
a vision that rouses
the people of a broken land.

Your fingers dream a nocturne,
andante con moto, lonely
like the ebb and flow of the tide,
trills tremble to be free.

From Danzig to Cracow, polonaise
stamps stricken memories.
Exiled maker of harmony, you pine
for the forests beyond the Vistula.

Do Rún

Táim loite le smaointe
tú ag siúl gan staonadh
timpeall is timpeall cearnóige
banaltra ar d'aire
de ló is d'oiche.

Is cuimhin liom tú tráthnóna
ag léamh cois fuinneóige
ór na gréine
ag lasadh do chuid gruaige
do aghaidh ag lonrú
lán de ghrá.

Ansin tú ar strae
ag maireachtáil i d'óìge
ag eirí eidtreórach
ag iarraidh éalú ó do phriosún
ag gearán gan staonadh
ag cur arraing trí ceartlár mo chléíbh.

Beirt inion
mo dheirfiúracha
marbh-bheirthe
rún do chrol san uaigh.

Your Secret
A version of Do Rún

I catch your eye, we hug,
you cover more laps
of the quadrangle

day and night trying to escape
from your prison
shooting arrows
through me.

I remember you reading
by the window
waves in your hair
gold in evening sun.

I see you
in your grandmother's eyes,
'the flower of the flock'
she wrote on the back of the photo.

A young bride
you smile from sepia;
your first born babies
my twin sisters.
Your silence.

Gealach na gCoinleach

M'athair ag baint prátai
den chré bog móintiúl
macalla fuaim spáide
mar shuantraí shéimh.

A dhrom tréan lúbtha
I dtreo ithtreach torthúla
a chos ag brú,
na prátai ag scaipeadh.

Seasann se dírech
sásamh an fhomhair ar a eadan
mise ar mo ghlúine i dteas na gréine
ag baillú bia an gheimhridh.

I gclap sholus súimid
I ngioracht a chéile
faoi iontas na cruinne.

Harvest Moon
A version of Gealach na gCoinleach

My father's spade
makes music digging
drills of peaty clay.

His back bends
to a rhythm as the spade sinks
then scatters potatoes in the air.

Standing still he smiles
in this Indian summer while
I gather baskets of cool potatoes.

A blood-red sun sinks
a harvest moon rises
we rest in the wonder of the universe.

Filthy Lucre

In the gold rush
of seventeen-ninety five
a teacher man
panning at night
finds a nugget.

News gets round
Croghan Mountain
gold fever seethes
in the river bed

the greedy hills
of Wicklow
will mint a fortune
for mountainy men.

Luke 1

Tiny suns
sparkle April gorse
swallows nest
in the barn's rafter
and you are one year old
lungs out-revving
dad's Yamaha.

From all fours
you ballet bandy legs
sit to press
Ernies's guitar button
clamber up
leap like Nureyev
a tearful tumble
a belly laugh.

Luke 2

Why are you afraid
         The dragon is outside
I'll give you the stars
to chase the dark away.

Why are you listening
         The wind is coming in
I'll play the tin whistle
to see the wind swing.

Where are you hiding
         I'm here far away
I'll run till I find you
if it takes all day.

Conor

Lifts an eyelid
Blinks open two
Eyes of hectic blue
Questions the sunlight
Slanting through

Like Alice he wonders
Agoos and agoos
Mouth open in a
Yawn like Daddy's

Or in a rosebud
Searching for a nipple
In the full moon
Of Mammy's breast.

Polly Perkins
For my daughter, Joanne

Icicles hang on the window pane
and Polly in jodhpurs
fills some oats in a pail
stretches to unlock the tack-room door.

Yellow sun glows on the cutstone gable
Lugnaquilla glimmers in its snowy thatch.
In high riding boots she runs to the stable,
cold hands grip the frosted latch.

A handful of oats for her Adonis
sunlight slants in a ray of gold
gripping his forelock, she his Venus,
jumps on his back and away they go.

I stand entranced under the stable awning
hear them gallop into the winter morning.

Horse Mirrored

O spirit shall I call you deity
or but a wandering being
from the ocean of the night
transcending to what you will.

Lover of the deep you canter
waves of seething spray,
rear to a blood red moon
struck by lunar ecstasy.

Let me drape you with
a wreath of wild olive leaf
fly to Phideas in Olympus
and sing the odes of Pindar.

The Space Between
after Barry Flanagan

Light on light
on sacks and stone
like Da Vinci
on Mona Lisa's skin.

Neolithic man
paints a deer in a cave,
you sketch a mermaid
cradling a hare.

Then fantasia spreads
to your antic hares –
lean bodies supple as Nijinsky's
all eyes, ears, tangents.

Apple Harvest

I see a smile
play in your eyes
listen for the clink of spade

wind-blown blossoms fade
crabbed fruit hides in leaf shadow

knarled knuckles twist
on blotch and pock of limb

apples hang heavy for dumplings
wasps and blackbirds gorge.

Leafless winter world
your bare bones sleep.

End of September

From the four corners of the wind,
Achill and Aran, Nephin and Muckish,
they travel in clusters, swapping symptoms,
boosting each other on their hesitant road
to the leafy suburb, where friends
of St. Luke's offer hope,
dry leaves and chestnuts crush under their feet.

Atlantic waves splash in the welcoming voice
of a white-coated nurse from the west.
She shows them their rooms where they rest
till the treatment begins in the clinic nearby.
Fears now diminished
they slope through the path,
dry leaves and chestnuts crush under their feet.

John King from Killalla,
his hair bleached by spray.
The life of the party waits in Wing A,
tattoos on his loins he lies on a table
longs for his fishing boat tied in the bay,
eddies of water lap under his feet.

Jack White comes from under Ben Bulben,
a whale of a man, he walks tall like a cowboy
in brown leather boots, his eyes smiling blue
and his beard like silk. Now bound by ice sheets
unable to sleep, he's back on his farm
loping its hills, a shepherd to his sheep,
gorse and heather crush under his feet.

Notes

Blessington Lakes (p.4). The word *forninth* means 'in front of'.

Landscape County Wicklow (p.11). The title of a painting by artist Evie Hone.

Your first love was Drogheda (p.17). For Alexander Williams RHA 1846 – 1930.

Passage Grave (p.22). Bettina Poeschel was a young German woman murdered in Co. Meath in 2001.

She chose the Rose. (p.29) This poem is dedicated to William Butler Yeats, one of the foremost figures of 20th century literature. Maud Gonne MacBride was an English-born Irish revolutionary and actress who had a turbulent relationship with Yeats.

Peaceable Kingdom Lost (p.36). The title refers to the book, *Peaceable Kingdom Lost. The Paxton Boys and the Destruction of William Penn's Holy Experiment* by Dr Kevin Kenny.

Wampum: traditional sacred shell beads of the indigenous people of North America. Often used by colonists as currency for trading with Native Americans.

St. Brigid (p.40). Brigid is the pagan goddess of Spring. In the Middle Ages, Brigid was syncretized with the Christian saint.

The Wave (p.46). This poem refers to the tsunami in Thailand in 2004.

Filthy Lucre (p.52). In 1795, there was a gold rush in County Wicklow and prospectors flocked to the Gold Mines River. Eighty kilograms of gold were recovered in just a few weeks, including a nugget weighing 682 grams, the largest single piece of gold found in Ireland and Britain.

Horse Mirrored (p.57). In 1996, the artist Barry Flanagan donated the sculpture *Horse, Mirrored* to The Hugh Lane Gallery, Dublin.